A Note From Rick Renner

I am on a personal quest to see a "revival of the Bible" so people can establish their lives on a firm foundation that will stand strong and endure the test as end-time storm winds begin to intensify.

In order to experience a revival of the Bible in your personal life, it is important to take time each day to read, receive, and apply its truths to your life. James tells us that if we will continue in the perfect law of liberty — refusing to be forgetful hearers, but determined to be doers — we will be blessed in our ways. As you watch or listen to the programs in this series and work through this corresponding study guide, I trust you will search the Scriptures and allow the Holy Spirit to help you hear something new from God's Word that applies specifically to your life. I encourage you to be a doer of the Word He reveals to you. Whatever the cost, I assure you — it will be worth it.

> Thy words were found, and I did eat them;
> and thy word was unto me the joy and rejoicing of mine heart:
> for I am called by thy name, O Lord God of hosts.
> — Jeremiah 15:16

Your brother and friend in Jesus Christ,

Rick Renner

How To Determine What God Gives and Never Gives

Copyright © 2021 by Rick Renner
P.O. Box 702040
Tulsa, OK 74170

Published by Rick Renner Ministries
www.renner.org

ISBN 13: 978-1-68031-960-6

eBook ISBN 13: 978-1-68031-961-3

How To Use This Study Guide

This five-lesson study guide corresponds to *"How To Determine What God Gives and Never Gives" With Rick Renner* (Renner TV). Each lesson in this study guide covers a topic that is addressed during the program series, with questions and references supplied to draw you deeper into your own private study of the Scriptures on this subject.

To derive the most benefit from this study guide, consider the following:

First, watch or listen to the program prior to working through the corresponding lesson in this guide. (Programs can also be viewed at **renner.org** by clicking on the Media/Archives links.)

Second, take the time to look up the scriptures included in each lesson. Prayerfully consider their application to your own life.

Third, use a journal or notebook to make note of your answers to each lesson's Study Questions and Practical Application challenges.

Fourth, invest specific time in prayer and in the Word of God to consult with the Holy Spirit. Write down the scriptures or insights He reveals to you.

Finally, take action! Whatever the Lord tells you to do according to His Word, do it.

For added insights on this subject, it is recommended that you obtain Rick Renner's book *A Life Ablaze: Ten Simple Keys To Living on Fire for God.* You may also select from Rick's other available resources by placing your order at **renner.org** or by calling 1-800-742-5593.

TOPIC

Introduction to James

SCRIPTURES

1. **James 1:1** — James, a servant of God and of the Lord Jesus Christ, to the twelve tribes which are scattered abroad, greeting.
2. **Matthew 13:55,56** — Is not this the carpenter's son? Is not his mother called Mary? And his brethren, James, and Joses, and Simon, and Judas? And his sisters, are they not all with us?....
3. **John 7:5** — For neither did his brethren believe in him.
4. **1 Corinthians 15:3-7** — For I delivered unto you first of all that which I also received, how that Christ died for our sins according to the scriptures; and that he was buried, and that he rose again the third day according to the scriptures: and that he was seen of Cephas, then of the twelve: after that, he was seen of above five hundred brethren at once; of whom the greater part remain unto this present, but some are fallen asleep. After that, he was seen of James....
5. **Romans 16:7** — Salute Andronicus and Junia, my kinsmen, and my fellow-prisoners, who are of note among the apostles, who also were in Christ before me.
6. **Acts 16:31** — And they said, Believe on the Lord Jesus Christ, and thou shalt be saved, and thy house.

GREEK WORDS

1. "servant" — δοῦλος (*doulos*): historically, one who was perpetually bound to do the bidding of his owner; this servant's existence was to service his master in whatever way the master asked or demanded; a slave whose principal task was to fulfill the desires of his master for the rest of his life; to help, assist, and fulfill his master's wants and dreams to the exclusion of all else; it is the picture of one whose will is completely swallowed up in the will of another
2. "Lord" — κύριος (*kurios*): lord, or supreme master
3. "Christ" — χριστός (*christos*): The Anointed One; the Messiah

SYNOPSIS

The five lessons in this study on *How To Determine What God Gives and Never Gives* will focus on the following topics:

- Introduction to James
- The Role of Joy
- The Role of Endurance
- Asking in Faith
- What God Gives and Never Gives

One of the most fascinating books in the New Testament is actually the oldest book of the New Testament. It is the short but powerful letter of James, and in its five chapters, there is much to learn and apply to our everyday living — including how to know what God gives and never gives.

The emphasis of this lesson:

James — who wrote the book of James — was the half-brother of Jesus and had three other brothers and at least two sisters. Although he was not a follower of Christ during His earthly ministry, James was radically saved after Jesus' resurrection and became the respected leader of the Church in Jerusalem. There he served the Lord faithfully up until the time of his death.

Who Is James?

James opens his letter by saying, "James, a servant of God and of the Lord Jesus Christ, to the twelve tribes which are scattered abroad, greeting" (James 1:1). The James that is writing here is the half-brother of Jesus. He and Jesus had the same mother, but they didn't have the same father. Jesus' Father was God, and James' father was Joseph.

It is interesting to note that when we study Scripture, we discover that Jesus had several siblings: four brothers and at least two sisters. Matthew 1:25 states that Mary and Joseph had no sexual relationship until after the birth of Jesus. Jesus was conceived supernaturally and was born as the Son of God. But after His birth, Mary and Joseph had a normal marital relationship, and they had several other children.

Their names are listed in Matthew 13:55 and 56, where the people of Nazareth contended, "Is not this the carpenter's son? Is not his mother called Mary? And his brethren, James, and Joses, and Simon, and Judas? And his sisters, are they not all with us?"

To be clear, Jesus was the firstborn Son of Mary and Joseph, and He was — and *is* — God in the flesh. James — who wrote the book of James — was their second-born. He was followed by his brother Joses, which is another name for Joseph, who was obviously named after their father. Simon was the third son, and Jude was fourth — who wrote the book of Jude. Thus, Jesus had four brothers, and according to Matthew 13:56 He also had "sisters." In Greek, this word is plural, which means there were at least two sisters but possibly more.

This was truly a remarkable family. It's interesting to note that Mary, the mother of Jesus, as well as His four brothers and His sisters were all in the Upper Room on the Day of Pentecost (*see* Acts 1:13,14). This means they were all filled with the Holy Spirit and spoke in tongues. Eventually, each member of Jesus' family became involved in ministry — but that was not the way they started out.

Rough Beginnings

The Bible tells us in John 7:5 that Jesus' brothers did not believe in Him during the course of His life. In fact, we know from early Church writings that James was antagonistic toward Jesus. Some may ask, "How could one grow up in the same household with Jesus and be His adversary?" Well, try to imagine what it would be like growing up in a family where your elder brother was God in the flesh. Jesus never did anything wrong and was always commended for doing everything right!

More than likely, James and his younger siblings were often compared to Jesus — perhaps regularly hearing the words, "Why can't you be more like Jesus?" Apparently, James was so fed up with living in the shadow of perfection that he developed resentment toward Jesus. Of course, Jesus was aware of the tension and turmoil in James, so when He was raised from the dead, He appeared to James personally. We find this fact recorded by Paul in his first letter to the Corinthian believers:

> **For I delivered unto you first of all that which I also received, how that Christ died for our sins according to the scriptures; and that he was buried, and that he rose again the third day**

according to the scriptures: and that he was seen of Cephas, then of the twelve: after that, he was seen of above five hundred brethren at once; of whom the greater part remain unto this present, but some are fallen asleep. After that, he was seen of James....

— 1 Corinthians 15:3-7

When James saw Jesus resurrected from the dead, he finally understood why his brother was so good. In that moment, he realized Jesus was more than just his brother — his brother was the Messiah, God in the flesh! It was at that time James was radically converted and not only became a believer but also the leader of the Church in Jerusalem.

His leadership role became so pivotal that we read about it in Acts 15. When the apostle Paul came to Jerusalem to explain to the leadership how the Gentiles were coming to Christ, it was James who mediated that conference (*see* Galatians 1:19). He was the leading voice in the city of Jerusalem at that time. You can imagine his level of notoriety simply because he was the natural-born brother of Jesus.

God Specializes in Calling Entire Families

Mary and Joseph raised a family that served in ministry. Jesus — their firstborn — was the Messiah. James became the head of the Church in Jerusalem and wrote the book of James. Jude was also very active and was the writer of Jude, the second to last book of the New Testament. Early Christian writers tell us Jesus' sisters were also involved in ministry.

Clearly, God is in the business of calling entire families to serve in His Kingdom. We see this pattern again and again in Scripture. Looking at the book of Genesis, we see:

- Noah, his wife, their three sons, and their wives were all called to fulfill God's plans.
- Abraham, Sarah, and their entire lineage were called.
- Isaac and Rebekah were selected by God to bring His will to the earth.
- Jacob and his twelve sons all played a part in God's purposes.
- Likewise, Moses, his brother Aaron, and their sister Miriam were called.

Then when we come to the New Testament, we see:

- Mary and Joseph and their children were all called into ministry.
- Zachariah, Elizabeth, and their son John the Baptist were called.
- James and John, "the sons of Zebedee," were called.
- Peter and Andrew, who were brothers, were also called to serve in Jesus' ministry.

Even the apostle Paul's family was called into God's service. As he closed his letter to the believers in Rome, he said, "Salute Andronicus and Junia, my kinsmen, and my fellow-prisoners, who are of note among the apostles, who also were in Christ before me" (Romans 16:7). The fact that he calls Andronicus and Junia his "kinsmen" indicates these were Paul's relatives, and they were born again *before* he became an apostle. This means there were three apostles in the same family.

Another family God called into ministry is that of Barnabas, whose name means the "son of encouragement." A careful reading of Acts 4 tells us that Barnabas was financially well off, and his extraordinary giving created a place for him among the apostles. He became a prophet, a teacher, and an apostle. His sister's name was Mary, and she was well-known among the Early Church. She had a very large apartment in Jerusalem with a huge room on the second or third floor — it's the space where the Day of Pentecost took place.

This same Mary — Barnabas' sister — had a son named John Mark who was also called into ministry. He accompanied his Uncle Barnabas and Paul on their first missionary journey and went on to become Peter's assistant that wrote down Peter's gospel, which we've come to know as the book of Mark. So in this one family, Barnabas, Mary, and John Mark were all called into ministry.

It All Starts With One Individual

When God saves entire families, His call is initiated with one person who has an encounter with Him and surrenders his life. Noah was the one in his family who first heard God's call and who developed the habit of walking with Him. Noah's decision affected his whole family and brought salvation to them.

Abraham was the one in his family who first heard and responded to God's invitation to follow Him. His decision affected his wife, Sarah, and their son Isaac, who pursued God after him. The call of entire families is actually a promise from God found in Acts 16:31, which says, "And they said, Believe on the Lord Jesus Christ, and thou shalt be saved, and thy house."

Although this verse doesn't mean everyone in your family will instantly be born again just because you get saved, it does promise that if you will believe on the Lord Jesus Christ and surrender your life to Him, your encounter with Him will be so impactful that eventually your whole family will come to Christ.

Make no mistake: God desires to save your entire family. He has a special assignment for you and each member of your family to accomplish.

The End of James' Life

Early Christian writers tell us James was the most visible believer in the city of Jerusalem toward the end of his life. He was often referred to as "James the just" and was said to have knees that looked like camel's knees. The reason for this was because he spent so many hours on his knees in prayer. He was loyally devoted to Christ and lived his life accordingly.

Since he was the most respected and influential believer in Jerusalem, the Jewish religious leaders tried to cut a deal with him. Basically, they said, "James, if you will renounce your faith in Jesus, your older brother, and declare Him to be a fraud, we'll promote you in every way we can. We'll give you power and great prestige." The Jewish leaders then lured James to the pinnacle of the temple — the same place the devil took Jesus when he tempted Him while in the desert.

This lets us know that the enemy is not very creative. He just keeps recycling the same temptations over and over again. That means when we learn the pattern of how Satan attacks, we can also learn how to avoid his traps and defeat him.

When James reached the pinnacle of the temple, the religious leaders told him to renounce Jesus. By this time, a crowd had gathered all around the temple base to hear what James would say. Instead of renouncing Jesus, James seized the moment to declare in effect, "This Jesus whom you have slain with wicked hands, God has raised back to life! He's no longer dead but alive and seated at the Father's right hand. In the future, He is going to come in the clouds of glory to judge the living and the dead."

Upon hearing James declare the lordship of Jesus, the religious leaders became infuriated and pushed him off the edge of the pinnacle of the temple, and he plummeted to the ground. There they beat him to death with clubs. James died in faith because he held tightly to the testimony of Jesus Christ, his Lord and Savior.

James Was a Sold-Out Servant of the Lord Jesus Christ!

Looking once more at James 1:1, it says, "James, a servant of God and of the Lord Jesus Christ, to the twelve tribes which are scattered abroad, greeting." The word "servant" here is the Greek word *doulos*, and it describes *one who was perpetually bound to do the bidding of his owner, a slave whose principal task is to fulfill the desires of his master for the rest of his life*. This servant would help, assist, and fulfill his master's wants and dreams to the exclusion of all else. His very existence was to service his master in whatever way the master asked or demanded. The word *doulos* is the picture of *one whose will is completely swallowed up in the will of another*.

By using the word *doulos* — translated here as "servant" — James was saying, "I'm a sold-out servant of God. I've surrendered everything I have, and I live for only one purpose — to do the will of God and the Lord Jesus Christ." James went from being antagonistic toward Jesus to fully surrendering His life to Him. In fact, James was so committed to Jesus that he called Him the "Lord, Jesus Christ."

In Greek, the word "Lord" is *kurios*, which means *lord* or *supreme master*. In the Septuagint — which is the Greek version of the Old Testament that James would have used — the word "Lord" (Kurios) is translated *Jehovah*. Therefore, when James called his older brother "Lord," he was calling Jesus *Jehovah*. He was literally declaring Jesus to be God in the flesh!

The name "Jesus" refers to His humanity and is the Greek rendering of the name *Joshua*, which means *savior*. The word "Christ" is the Greek word *christos*, and it is the term that describes *the Anointed One, the Messiah*. So when James wrote the phrase "The Lord Jesus Christ," he was declaring Jesus as *Jehovah in the flesh*. Likewise, every time you say, "Lord Jesus

Christ," you are also declaring Jesus as Jehovah God in the flesh — the Anointed One, the Messiah.

Friend, Jesus was not just a prophet or a good man that lived 2,000 years ago. He is *the Lord Jesus Christ*! And just as James was His servant, we too are called to be His servants in this life.

STUDY QUESTIONS

Study to shew thyself approved unto God, a workman that needeth not to be ashamed, rightly dividing the word of truth.
— 2 Timothy 2:15

1. What new insights did you learn about James — during his early years as well as his latter days? How about Jesus and the family He grew up in?

2. Does God want to save everyone in your family? Carefully read what the Bible says in First Timothy 2:1-4 and Acts 16:31 and write what God has to say about it. What part do *you* play in seeing your loved ones come to Christ?

3. Jesus was the ultimate example of what it means to be a *servant* (*doulos*) of God! Carefully reflect on His actions recorded in John 13:3-17 and Philippians 2:3-8 and write down what the Holy Spirit speaks to you about being a true servant of God like Jesus.

PRACTICAL APPLICATION

But be ye doers of the word, and not hearers only, deceiving your own selves.
— James 1:22

1. Imagine *you* were James. What would your life have been like if you grew up having Jesus — who is God in the flesh — as your elder brother? What do you think you would have struggled with most?

2. We see a definite pattern in Scripture of how God specializes in calling entire families into His Kingdom. Who in your family has God saved and how are they serving the Lord? What family members does God seem to be working on? Pray that their spiritual eyes will be opened to the truth and that God will give them the measure of faith

they need to believe in and receive Jesus as their Savior and Lord (*see* 2 Corinthians 4:3-6; Romans 12:3).

3. Satan tempted James in a very similar way he tempted Jesus when He was in the wilderness, which tells us he's not very creative. He just keeps recycling the same temptations again and again. What pattern can you see in the way Satan attacks *you* and *your family*? Pray and ask God to reveal the enemy's recurring temptations and what you can do to avoid his traps and defeat him.

LESSON 2

TOPIC
The Role of Joy

SCRIPTURES

1. **James 1:1** — James, a servant of God and of the Lord Jesus Christ, to the twelve tribes which are scattered abroad, greeting.

2. **Acts 8:1** — And Saul was consenting unto his death. And at that time there was a great persecution against the church which was at Jerusalem; and they were all scattered abroad throughout the regions of Judaea and Samaria, except the apostles.

3. **Romans 6:11** — Likewise reckon ye also yourselves to be dead indeed unto sin, but alive unto God through Jesus Christ our Lord.

4. **Luke 10:30** — And Jesus answering said, A certain man went down from Jerusalem to Jericho, and fell among thieves, which stripped him of his raiment, and wounded him, and departed, leaving him half dead.

GREEK WORDS

1. "scattered abroad" — διασπορά (*diaspora*): the random scattering of seed; used to depict the scattering of Jewish believers

2. "great" — μέγας (*megas*) big, great, huge, or enormous

3. "persecution" — διώκω (*dioko*): to pursue; to follow after; to persecute; pictures the actions of a hunter who followed after an animal to apprehend, capture, and kill it

4. "scattered abroad"— διασπορά (*diaspora*): the random scattering of seed; used to depict the scattering of Jewish believers

5. "brethren"— ἀδελφός (*adelphos*): a term used to describe two or more who were born from the same womb; an endearing term used to describe those of one's own family; later used in a military sense to depict brothers in battle; a comrade; hence, brotherhood

6. "count it"— ἡγέομαι (*hegeomai*): to reckon; to determine; pictures a determination not left to chance

7. "joy"— χαρά (*chara*): joy, not happiness

8. "when"— ὅταν (*hotan*): subjunctive, whenever, probably unpredictable

9. "ye fall"— περιπίπτω (*peripipto*): pictures falling into a deep ditch; in context, to be completely surrounded by encompassing problems

SYNOPSIS

As we saw in our first lesson, James was the half-brother of Jesus. They both had the same mother — Mary — but they didn't have the same father. James' father was Joseph, and Jesus' Father was God Himself. In addition to James, Jesus had at least two sisters and three other brothers named Joses, Simon, and Judas (*see* Matthew 13:55,56).

What's interesting about James 1:1 is that James identifies himself as a servant of the "Lord Jesus Christ," which is the very first time this title is written in print. By using these words, he was declaring Jesus to be *Jehovah God in the flesh*. Likewise, every time you say, "Lord Jesus Christ," you are also declaring Jesus to be Jehovah God in the flesh — the Anointed One, the Messiah!

The emphasis of this lesson:

The book of James was originally written to suffering believers scattered throughout the Roman Empire as a result of great persecution. James referred to them as his 'brothers' and expressed that he was proud of them. Although unexpected satanic attacks are going to come, we are to decide in advance to tap into the supernatural joy of the Holy Spirit deep within us to carry us through to victory.

Who Was James Writing to?

In the opening verse of James' letter, we discover to whom he's writing. He addressed his words "...to the twelve tribes which are scattered abroad..." (James 1:1). The phrase "scattered abroad" is very important. It is the Greek word *diaspora*, which describes *the random scattering of seed*. Here, this word was used to depict *the scattering of Jewish believers*.

In the First Century world, seed was either planted in a nice, neat row one seed at a time or it was scattered randomly. The word *diaspora* describes this *random scattering*. The sower would reach his hand into a satchel of seed, grab a handful, and then randomly scatter it over a field, throwing a little here and a little there.

This is a picture of what happened to believers in the First Century. Like seed seized by the hand of the sower, they were taken away from family and friends, removed from their homes and jobs, and randomly scattered all over the eastern lands of the Mediterranean without rhyme or reason. This tells us the displacement of these believers was not nice, neat, or orderly; it was very disruptive and chaotic.

A Great Persecution
Produced a Great Dispersion of Believers

The death of Stephen at the hands of the religious leaders marked the beginning of this dispersion and increased persecution against the Church. This is recorded in Acts 8:1, which says, "And Saul was consenting unto his [Stephen's] death. And at that time there was a great persecution against the church which was at Jerusalem; and they were all scattered abroad throughout the regions of Judaea and Samaria, except the apostles."

The word "great" in this verse is the Greek word *megas*, which describes *something big, great, huge, or enormous*. This tells us the persecution against the Church was *enormous*. The word "persecution" is the Greek word *dioko*, and it can be used negatively or positively. It means *to pursue, to follow after*, or *to persecute*. It was the term used to describe *the actions of a hunter who followed after an animal to apprehend, capture, and kill it*.

This "great persecution" was led by Saul — who later became the apostle Paul. It was a house-to-house hunt launched throughout Jerusalem. Like animals aggressively tracked by hunters, Christians ran for their lives to escape the murderous clutches of Saul and the religious leaders. This persecution is what caused believers to be "scattered abroad," which is the Greek word *diaspora*, describing the random scattering of seed — the same word used in James 1:1 to describe the scattering of Jewish believers. It was to these suffering Christians that James addressed his letter.

James Called His Readers 'Brothers'

James begins his instruction to the scattered believers in verse 2 by saying, "My brethren, count it all joy when ye fall into divers temptations." Take note of what he calls his readers — "my brethren." This word "brethren" is a translation of the Greek word *adelphos*, which is a form of the word *delphos*, the word for *a woman's womb*. When an "a" is placed in front of *delphos*, it describes *two or more who were born from the same womb*. This was an endearing term used to describe *those of one's own family*.

What's interesting about this word *adelphos*, translated "brethren," was that it was later used in a military sense to depict *brothers in battle, comrades*, or a *brotherhood*. It was first made popular by Alexander the Great, notably one of the greatest soldiers in human history. Every soldier wanted to be affiliated with Alexander. So from time to time, he would host a huge award ceremony and call especially brave soldiers up on the stage to stand with him. He'd then wrap his arm around the soldier who had been especially brave, and in front of all the other soldiers, Alexander would call the soldier next to him *adelphos*. It was his way of saying, "Brother, you and I are in this fight together!" Hence, the word *adelphos* carried the idea of camaraderie and was the greatest honor that could be conferred upon a soldier.

James understood the meaning of this word, and by using it, he was telling his readers that he was proud of them. In addition to being "born from the same spiritual womb" and being related in Christ, James was declaring that they were fellow fighters together. Even though they were struggling, this highly respected Christian leader symbolically wrapped his arm around them and let them know he was honored to be fighting the good fight of faith right alongside them.

Instead of condemning them for struggling in their faith because of the persecution they were experiencing, he voiced that he was pleased that they were still in the fight. In the same way, we need to reach out to our "fellow soldiers" and encourage them for not giving up despite the difficulties they're facing. If they are still taking one step at a time and they haven't quit, we need to let them know how proud we are of them — just as James did for the believers in the Early Church.

He Told Them To *Decide in Advance* How They Would Respond to Difficulties

After celebrating their tenacity for sticking it out in the midst of great trouble, James told his readers to "…Count it all joy…" (James 1:2). The words "count it" are a translation of the Greek word *hegeomai*, which means *to reckon* or *to determine*. It pictures *a determination not left to chance*. Thus, when James said, "Count it all joy," he was essentially saying, "Determine to have joy — make a decision to be in joy. Don't leave it to your feelings or chance."

This same Greek word *hegeomai* is also used in Romans 6:11, which says, "Likewise reckon ye also yourselves to be dead indeed unto sin, but alive unto God through Jesus Christ our Lord." The word "reckon" in this verse is the Greek word *hegeomai*, which means when sin tries to show up in your life, rather than tolerate it or just hope it goes away, you need to reckon it dead. That is, *make a decision* not to let it operate in your life. At the same time, you are to reckon yourself alive unto God. Don't waver or leave it to chance.

The word *hegeomai* depicts *a predetermined course of action — a decision not left to emotions or circumstances*. By using this word, James essentially told his readers, "You need to make a decision that you're going to have joy in your life regardless of what you're experiencing. It's not just going to happen automatically. You need to decide on it."

There's a Big Difference Between 'Joy' and 'Happiness'

What predetermined course of action were they to take? James said, "My brethren, count it all joy when ye fall into divers temptations" (James 1:2). Now James didn't say, "Enjoy all your problems," or, "Try to be happy when you fall into divers temptations." He said, "Make a predetermined decision to have joy, even in the most difficult situations."

The key to having joy is found in understanding what the word "joy" actually means. It is the Greek word *chara*, which describes *joy, not happiness*.

This word *chara* is a derivative of the word *charis*, which is the Greek word for *grace*. Therefore, when the Bible talks about *joy*, it is talking about a quality produced supernaturally deep inside of us by the grace of God. It is not determined by what's happening around us or by what we feel.

Happiness is connected with what's *happening* around us. It is like the ripples on the surface of a lake or river. The top of the water is affected by the environment and atmospheric conditions, and it is changing all the time. One day it's smooth, and the next day it's rough. However, down near the bottom of that lake or river, the water conditions stay virtually unchanged. Regardless of what's happening on the surface, the inside core remains steady and consistent.

That is what joy is like — it is *unchanging*. God doesn't want us to live like the water on the surface, constantly moved by what is happening in our environment. When circumstances are good, we're happy, but when they're bad, we're unhappy. He wants us to live deeper like the current on the bottom of the lake or river — He wants us to have joy.

Happiness is a fleeting emotion that comes and goes, but joy is a work of grace produced by the Holy Spirit deep inside us. It remains the same regardless of what's happening in our lives. Choosing joy is the first step to getting out of any trap the enemy has set for us. This is an inner determination that says, "I'm no longer going to be swayed by circumstances, nor am I going to follow the ups and downs of my emotions. I'm going to jump into the current of supernatural joy deep inside me, and it's going to carry me out of this dark place to where God wants me to be."

Choose Joy
'When Ye Fall into Divers Temptations'

Note that James said we are to count it all joy "...*when* ye fall into divers temptations" (James 1:2). The word "when" here is the Greek word *hotan*, which is subjunctive and means it is probably *something unpredictable* that is going to take you off guard or by surprise. That's how we're attacked by the enemy — unexpectedly and by surprise, and this happens to all of us. James didn't say, "*If* you fall into temptations" — he said *when*.

This brings us to the phrase "ye fall" — a translation of the Greek word *peripipto*, which is a compound of the words *peri* and *pipto*. The word *peri* means *around* and describes *a circle*; and the word *pipto* means *to fall head first.* When these words are compounded to form the word *peripipto,* it pictures *a person falling into a deep ditch and realizing he is completely surrounded by encompassing problems on every side.*

This word is only used one other place in the New Testament, and it is in the story of the Good Samaritan. Luke 10:30 says, "And Jesus answering said, A certain man went down from Jerusalem to Jericho, and fell among thieves, which stripped him of his raiment, and wounded him, and departed, leaving him half dead." The phrase "fell among" is this same Greek word *peripipto.* The man traveling was surrounded on all sides by thieves, and they stripped him, robbed him, wounded him, and left him for dead.

James' use of this word *peripipto* — translated here as "ye fall" — tells us that the divers temptations *we fall* into are major hardships that *strip us, rob us, wound us,* and even *leave us half-dead.* James said, "When you fall into these kinds of disastrous events, make a decision to jump into that deeper flow of joy." In other words, by the power of the Holy Spirit living in you, choose not to be affected by the circumstances on the surface.

The attitude of joy will take you into the victory that Jesus has planned for your life.

The truth is, no matter how long we have walked with God or how spiritual we are, all of us experience a "when" moment of attack when the enemy throws a calculated test our way that takes us completely by surprise. James calls these attacks "divers temptations," and the believers he was writing to were wondering if they were from God. In our upcoming lessons, we will see the true source of the assaults we face and how we are to respond to them.

STUDY QUESTIONS

> Study to shew thyself approved unto God, a workman that
> needeth not to be ashamed, rightly dividing the word of truth.
> — 2 Timothy 2:15

1. According to God's Word, where does joy come from and why is this supernatural fruit so vital in your life?
   - **You receive joy from…** [*see* Psalm 16:11; Jeremiah 15:16; John 15:7-11; 16:24].

- **Joy is vital because...** [*see* Nehemiah 8:10; 1 Thessalonians 5:16-18; 1 Peter 4:12,13].

In your own words, what would you say is the difference between *happiness* and the supernatural *joy* of God? What is happiness based on that has nothing to do with the source of joy? Which do you tend to live out of more — happiness or joy?

Having and holding onto joy in the middle of a mess of problems is not natural — it's *supernatural* and requires the supernatural work of the Holy Spirit living in you. Take a few moments to meditate on these passages and use them to create a personal daily prayer asking God to cultivate, generate, and release His joy in your life. [Isaiah 40:28-31; Psalm 28:7,8; 46:1-5; 84:4-12; Philippians 4:13; Jude 20]

PRACTICAL APPLICATION

But be ye doers of the word, and not hearers only,
deceiving your own selves.
—James 1:22

1. Imagine *you* were one of the believers who was "scattered abroad" during the First Century. What do you think your life would have been like had you been taken away from family and friends, removed from your home and job, and randomly scattered to a distant place? How might you prepare yourself — and your family — should an event like this occur today?

2. James was the most highly respected Christian leader in Jerusalem, and through his letter, he symbolically wrapped his arm around the Christians who were suffering and let them know how proud he was to be fighting the good fight of faith with them. Who has encouraged you in this way when you were going through a tough time? Look around you — who can you reach out to and encourage with a letter, a phone call, or a personal visit?

3. Have you fallen (*peripipto*) into a deep ditch and realize you're completely surrounded by problems on every side? What exactly are you dealing with? How is this lesson encouraging and equipping you to **make a predetermined decision** (*hegeomai*) that you're going **to choose joy** in your life regardless of your circumstances or how you are feeling?

TOPIC

The Role of Endurance

SCRIPTURES

1. **James 1:2-5** — My brethren, count it all joy when ye fall into divers temptations; Knowing this, that the trying of your faith worketh patience. But let patience have her perfect work, that ye may be perfect and entire, wanting nothing. If any of you lack wisdom, let him ask of God, that giveth to all men liberally, and upbraideth not....

2. **Luke 10:30** — And Jesus answering said, A certain man went down from Jerusalem to Jericho, and fell among thieves, which stripped him of his raiment, and wounded him, and departed, leaving him half dead.

GREEK WORDS

1. "when" — ὅταν (*hotan*): subjunctive, whenever, probably unpredictable

2. "ye fall" — περιπίπτω (*peripipto*): pictures falling into a deep ditch; in context, to be completely surrounded by encompassing problems

3. "divers" — ποικίλος (*poikilos*): divers, diversity; variety; multicolored

4. "temptations" — πειράζω (*peiradzo*): to test, try, or tempt; to cause one to fail, to falter, to stumble, or to bring destruction; depicts a calculated test to bring about failure; used to denote the actions of the devil, the tempter, or of the Pharisees and Sadducees

5. "trying" — δοκιμάζω (*dokimadzo*): pictures the process of testing a product to see if it can live up to its reputation; to determine the quality of a thing; to determine if a product or claim is as good as it is asserted to be; to authenticate; to prove

6. "worketh" — κατεργάζομαι (*katergadzomai*): to work down from the top to the bottom; to thoroughly work throughout

7. "patience" — ὑπομονή (*hupomone*): pictures defiantly sticking it out regardless of pressures mounted against it; staying power; "hang-in-there" power; the attitude that holds out, holds on, outlasts, perseveres, and hangs in there, never giving up, refusing to surrender to obstacles,

and turning down every opportunity to quit; pictures one who is under a heavy load, but refuses to give up or surrender

8. "perfect" — τέλειον (*teleion*): mature; graduating up to the next level

9. "entire" — ὀλόκληρος (*holokleros*): depicts possessing everything allotted to one by inheritance

10. "wanting nothing" — λείπω (*leipo*): a deficiency of any type; here, having no deficiency of any type

11. "lack" — λείπω (*leipo*): a deficiency of any type

12. "wisdom" — σοφός (*sophos*): wisdom not naturally attained; special insight

13. "ask" — αἰτέω (*aiteo*): to request, beseech, petition, or demand; to ask with full expectation of receiving what was firmly requested

14. "of" — παρὰ (*para*): alongside

15. "giveth" — τοῦ διδόντος Θεοῦ (*tou didontos Theou*): of the giving God; the God that giveth

16. "liberally" — ἁπλῶς (*haplos*): something given generously, abundantly, plentifully, profusely, bountifully, and open-handedly; copiously, amply, extravagantly, lavishly, liberally, plentifully, or richly; can also mean directly, simply, or sincerely

17. "upbraideth" — ὀνειδίζω (*oneididzo*): to nitpick

SYNOPSIS

So far in our study, we have seen that James, the half-brother of Jesus, has written his letter to the believers who have been scattered like seed all across the eastern lands of the Roman Empire. A great persecution had come against the Church, and the attack was so intense that the people were wondering if God was the One sending it — or at least allowing it to take place in their lives.

Since James was the leader of the Church in Jerusalem, the believers respectfully reached out to him with their questions and concerns. The book of James is his response of encouragement.

The emphasis of this lesson:

James instructs us to "count it all joy" when we face all kinds of difficult tests and temptations. This predetermined decision to hold onto joy in spite of our circumstances or feelings is a choice to live on the deeper

level of the Spirit. It attracts God's supernatural empowerment, cultivating the divine endurance we need to be able to get out of the ditch and walk in victory. When God's patience is allowed to fully mature us, we will be lacking in nothing.

What Does It Mean To 'Count It All Joy'?

Knowing the believers were facing a barrage of attacks, James began by saying, "My brethren, count it all joy when ye fall into divers temptations" (James 1:2). There are several key words in this verse we noted in Lesson 2, including the word "when." In Greek, this is the word *hotan*, which is subjunctive and indicates that attacks are often *unpredictable* and will probably take you by surprise. The use of the word "when" (*hotan*) signifies that these satanic attacks will come to all of us at a time we least expect it.

In those unexpected moments, James urged his readers — including *us* — to "count it all joy." We have seen that this word "count" is the Greek word *hegeomai*, which means *to reckon* or *to determine*. It pictures *a predetermined decision not left to chance* — a decision that says, "I don't care what happens or what difficult circumstances come my way. I'm not going to give in! I'm going to hold onto joy."

We saw that "joy" is the Greek word *chara*, which describes *joy, not happiness*. This word *chara* is derived from the word *charis*, which is the Greek word for *grace*. Therefore, when the Bible talks about *joy*, it is talking about *a quality produced supernaturally deep inside our hearts by the grace of God*. It is not determined by what's happening around us or by what we feel. When we make a predetermined choice to live on the deeper, undisturbed level of joy, we are choosing to walk in victory.

The Supernatural Energy of Joy Pulls Us Out of the Ditch and Into Victory

When are we to make this predetermined decision to hold tightly to joy? James said, "...When ye fall into divers temptations" (James 1:2). The phrase "ye fall" here is a translation of the Greek word *peripipto*, which is a compound of the words *peri* and *pipto*. The word *peri* describes *a circle* or *something that surrounds you*; and the word *pipto* means *to fall head first*. When these words are joined to form the new word *peripipto*, it describes *an all-encompassing problem that surrounds us.* It is the picture of a person who has fallen head first into a deep ditch, and when he gets up, he finds himself completely surrounded by encompassing problems on every side.

We noted that this word *peripipto* is only used one other place in the New Testament, and that is in the story of the Good Samaritan found in Luke 10:30. Here the Bible says, "And Jesus answering said, A certain man went down from Jerusalem to Jericho, and fell among thieves, which stripped him of his raiment, and wounded him, and departed, leaving him half dead."

The phrase "fell among" here is *peripipto* — the same Greek word translated as "fall" in James 1:2. Jesus said this man was surrounded on all sides by thieves, and they stripped him, robbed him, wounded him, and left him for dead. The fact that James used this same word tells us that the "divers temptations" he talked about are major hardships that *strip you, rob you, wound you,* and even *leave you half dead.* When you fall into these kinds of disastrous events, make a decision to jump into that deeper flow of joy. The attitude of joy will take you into the victory that Jesus has planned for your life.

'Divers Temptations'

James said we are to tap into the current of joy when we fall into "divers temptations" (James 1:2). The Greek word for "divers" is *poikilos,* which means *divers* or *diversity.* It describes a *variety* or *something multicolored* and is the same word used in the Greek Septuagint in Genesis 37 to describe Joseph's coat of "many" colors.

Therefore, when James said, "...Count it all joy when ye fall into divers temptations," he let us know that the devil's temptations are *"multicolored."* In other words, they come in *all shapes and sizes,* so don't think they're always going to be the same. Nevertheless, whatever he sends our way, we have the God-given ability to overcome it because the Greater One lives inside us (*see* 1 John 4:4).

This brings us to the word "temptations" — the Greek word *peiradzo,* which means *to test, try, or tempt.* It is *something that causes one to fail, to falter, to stumble,* or *to bring destruction.* This word *peiradzo* depicts *a calculated test to bring about failure,* and it was used to denote the actions of the devil, the tempter, as well as the Pharisees and Sadducees when they came against Jesus.

An example of the word *peiradzo* (temptations) is seen when the devil brought a calculated test against Jesus in the wilderness (*see* Luke 4:1-13). Satan also worked through the Jewish leaders, bringing questions, arguments, and accusations against Jesus throughout His ministry to try to entrap Him and ruin His reputation. The word *peiradzo* denotes *a premeditated attack* and carries the idea of being crushed, devastated, and destroyed. This describes what many believers were experiencing during the time of persecution in the First Century.

The 'Trying of Your Faith Worketh Patience'

James goes on to say, "Knowing this, that the trying of your faith worketh patience" (James 1:3). The words "knowing this" is a participle, which means it would be better translated as *knowing, knowing, knowing, knowing, knowing*. It carries the idea of always knowing something, never losing sight of it nor forgetting it. It is a continuous and uninterrupted action. What is it that we're supposed to know and keep on knowing and never ever forget? James said, "...That the trying of your faith worketh patience" (James 1:3).

The word "trying" here is very significant. It is the Greek word *dokimadzo*, which pictures *the process of testing a product to see if it can live up to its reputation*. It means *to determine the quality of a thing* or *to determine if a product or claim is as good as it is asserted to be*. Essentially, this word *dokimadzo* carries the idea of authenticating or proving something.

For example, if someone had a product and advertised about how great it was, they would vigorously test it to see if it was everything it was advertised to be. That is what the word *dokimadzo* means. It describes *the process of authentication*.

That's what happens in our Christian walk. When we move into a position of faith and begin to declare things like, "By Jesus' stripes I'm healed, and I'm going to walk in divine health," the enemy hears our words and sees our stance and decides to come and test us to see if what we're claiming is accurate and true. His goal is to get us to move out of our position of faith. Each test he brings is our opportunity to authenticate and prove that our faith is real. That is what this phrase "trying of your faith" means.

At the same time the enemy is testing your faith, God is working patience into you. The word "worketh" in James 1:3 is the Greek word *katergadzomai*, which means *to work down from the top to the bottom*. It depicts *something that is thoroughly worked throughout.* This word "worketh" describes a person who has been supernaturally energized. When you choose to push back against the enemy's attack, a divine empowerment takes place, which begins at the top of your head and works its way down to your feet. God joins Himself to you and releases in you an empowerment that the Bible calls "patience."

This word "patience" is the Greek word *hupomone*, which is the compound of the words *hupo* and *meno.* The word *hupo* means *under* and depicts *one under a very heavy load*; and the word *meno* is *the resolve to stay put, abide,* and *not move.* When these two words are compounded, the word *hupomone* pictures *one who defiantly sticks it out regardless of pressures mounted against it.* It is *staying power* or *"hang-in-there" power.* It is *the attitude that holds out, holds on, outlasts, perseveres, and hangs in there, never giving up, refusing to surrender to obstacles, and turning down every opportunity to quit.*

According to James 1:3, when the enemy comes to test you and prove your faith and you push back against his attack, that's when God joins Himself to you and supernaturally releases the empowerment of *hupomone* — translated here as "patience" — into your life. This divine power — *hupomone* — to outlast the enemy would better be translated as *endurance* and was actually viewed by the Early Church as the queen of all virtues. Even though they were experiencing an intense attack, they knew if they had *hupomone* (endurance), it wasn't a question of *if* they would win, but *when* they would win. The same holds true for you!

Patience Produces Spiritual Maturity

The Bible goes on to say, "But let patience have her perfect work, that ye may be perfect and entire, wanting nothing" (James 1:4). This verse lets us know that to stay in our place of faith is *hard work.* Through James, God is telling us to allow patience (*hupomone*) to "have her perfect work" within us. This word "perfect" is the Greek word *teleion,* which describes *maturity* and depicts *one graduating from one level up to the next level.* When you stand in faith and exercise your trust in God, you become spiritually developed and moved into higher levels of faith.

In addition to becoming mature, James also said you would be "entire," which is the Greek word *holokleros,* and it means *possessing everything allotted to one by inheritance.* It denotes *a family or an individual who possesses everything originally allotted by inheritance.* The word *holokleros* is a picture of one who hasn't lost anything that has been given to him. He is standing in his full inheritance.

As a believer, your inheritance includes everything you have received through Christ's work of redemption on the Cross, such as His healing, deliverance, prosperity, peace, joy, healthy relationships, and countless other blessings. When "patience" (*hupomone*) has its way in your life, the Bible says you will be "wanting nothing." In Greek, "wanting nothing" is a form of the Greek word *leipo*, which describes *a deficiency of any type*. In this verse, it means *having no deficiency of any type*.

If You Need Wisdom, Ask God for It

Now you may be thinking, *I've been standing in faith and standing in faith for a very long time, and I still haven't received the manifestation of what God promised. In fact, I'm still under attack. Why isn't this working in my life?* That's a good question — and one that many of us have asked at certain times in our lives.

The people James was writing to were asking him the same question. What advice did he give them? It's found in James 1:5: If any of you lack wisdom, let him ask of God, that giveth to all men liberally, and upbraideth not...."

Notice the word "lack." It is again the Greek word *leipo*, and it describes *a deficiency of any type*. In this case, James is specifically saying if you *lack* or *have a deficiency of wisdom*, ask God for it. This word "wisdom" in Greek is the word *sophos*, and it describes *wisdom not naturally attained; special insight*. If you need wisdom for any situation you're facing, James said, "Ask of God."

The word "ask" is the Greek word *aiteo*, which means *to request, beseech, petition,* or *demand*. It carries the idea of *asking with full expectation of receiving what was firmly requested*. What's interesting is even the word "of" is important. It is the Greek word *para*, and it means *alongside*. God will tell you anything you need to know *about Him, about you,* or *about the situations and people with which you are dealing*. But His one stipulation to receiving wisdom regarding your situation is that you come *alongside* (*para*) Him.

God Is Generous, Not Stingy, With Everything He Gives

Please realize that **God is the God of the open hand — not a clenched fist**. He's not saying, "I have all the answers you need, but I don't know if I'm going to give them to you unless you beg Me enough." That's not how God operates. He said through James, "If any of you lack wisdom, let him ask of God, that giveth..." (James 1:5). In the original Greek, it actually says, "...Ask of *the giving God*...." or "the God that giveth."

How does God give? James 1:5 says He "...giveth to all men liberally, and upbraideth not...." The word "liberally" is the Greek word *haplos*, which describes *something given generously, abundantly, plentifully, profusely, bountifully, and open-handedly*. It depicts *something provided copiously, amply, extravagantly, lavishly, liberally, plentifully, or richly*. The word *haplos* can also mean *directly, simply, or sincerely*.

If you lack wisdom, ask of the giving God, who will *lavishly* and *profusely* give you the insight you need "...and upbraideth not..." (James 1:5). The word "upbraideth" here is the Greek word *oneididzo*, which means *to nitpick*. This verse is clearly declaring that *God is not a nitpicker* who is waiting to point out all your faults and weaknesses. If you will come alongside (*para*) Him for help in your situation, He will open His hand and generously give you what you need. He is your Father, and you are His child who He loves dearly!

STUDY QUESTIONS

> **Study to shew thyself approved unto God, a workman that needeth not to be ashamed, rightly dividing the word of truth.**
> **— 2 Timothy 2:15**

1. The devil brought "temptations" (*peiradzo*) against Jesus when He was in the wilderness fasting and seeking God for 40 days. What can you learn from Jesus' response and apply in your life when the enemy brings a calculated test against you? (*See* Matthew 4:1-11; Luke 4:1-13.)

2. What specific promise (or promises) from God's Word are you tenaciously standing on and holding onto right now? Take a moment and

right them out and declare them out loud in faith over your life, over your situations, and against the enemy.

3. The Bible says, "[God] disarmed the principalities and powers that were ranged against us and made a bold display and public example of them, in triumphing over them in Him and in it [the cross]" (Colossians 2:15 *AMPC*). Take some time to really "chew" on this verse and this passage from Isaiah.

"But no weapon that is formed against you shall prosper, and every tongue that shall rise against you in judgment you shall show to be in the wrong. This [peace, righteousness, security, triumph over opposition] is **the heritage of the servants of the Lord** [those in whom the ideal Servant of the Lord is reproduced]..." (Isaiah 54:17 *AMPC*).

How do these scriptures strengthen you to stay in your place of faith until you see God's promises fulfilled in your life?

PRACTICAL APPLICATION

But be ye doers of the word, and not hearers only,
deceiving your own selves.
—James 1:22

1. Look back over your life and recall a time when you experienced a "trying of your faith." Describe the test the enemy brought against you. How did God use that test to develop divine endurance (patience) in your character?

2. How did God ultimately bring you through/deliver you from the above situation? How does the memory of God's powerful hand at work in your life encourage you to hang on and trust Him to bring you out of the current difficulties you're facing?

3. James said, "If any of you lacks wisdom, you should ask God, who gives generously to all without finding fault, and it will be given to you" (James 1:5 *NIV*). What situations do you need supernatural wisdom for right now? Take a few moments to pray and ask God for the insight you need.

TOPIC

Asking in Faith

SCRIPTURES

1. **James 1:2-5** — My brethren, count it all joy when ye fall into divers temptations; Knowing this, that the trying of your faith worketh patience. But let patience have her perfect work, that ye may be perfect and entire, wanting nothing. If any of you lack wisdom, let him ask of God, that giveth to all men liberally, and upbraideth not; and it shall be given.

2. **James 1:6-8** — But let him ask in faith, nothing wavering. For he that wavereth is like a wave of the sea driven with the wind and tossed. For let not that man think that he shall receive any thing of the Lord. A double minded man is unstable in all his ways.

3. **James 1:9-12** — Let the brother of low degree rejoice in that he is exalted: But the rich, in that he is made low: because as the flower of the grass he shall pass away. For the sun is no sooner risen with a burning heat, but it withereth the grass, and the flower thereof falleth, and the grace of the fashion of it perisheth: so also shall the rich man fade away in his ways. Blessed is the man that endureth temptation: for when he is tried, he shall receive the crown of life, which the Lord hath promised to them that love him.

GREEK WORDS

1. "of" — παρὰ (*para*): alongside
2. "of God that giveth" — τοῦ διδόντος Θεοῦ (*tou didontos Theou*): of the giving God; the God that giveth
3. "to all" — πᾶσιν (*pasin*): to all; an all-inclusive term with no exceptions
4. "liberally" — ἁπλῶς (*haplos*): something given generously, abundantly, plentifully, profusely, bountifully, and open-handedly; copiously, amply, extravagantly, lavishly, liberally, plentifully, or richly
5. "upbraideth" — ὀνειδίζω (*oneididzo*): to nitpick
6. "but" — δέ (*de*): a marker to indicate something important; however

7. "ask" — αἰτέω (*aiteo*): to request, petition, or demand; to ask with full expectation of receiving what was firmly requested

8. "in" — ἐν (*en*): in; being rooted in; from a position of being in

9. "wavering" — διακρινόμενος (*diakrinomenos*): habitual vacillation

10. "wave" — κλύδωνι (*kludoni*): one wave after another wave, a succession of rising and falling waves

11. "driven with the wind" — ἀνεμίζω (*anemidzo*): driven along by the push of the wind; agitated and stirred up by the movement of wind

12. "tossed" — ῥιπίζω (*rhipidzo*): constantly or habitually rising and falling, like the ever-changing positions of waves in the sea

13. "double-minded" — δίψυχος (*dipsuchos*): two-souled; double-minded; pictures one who vacillates back and forth constantly

14. "unstable" — ἀκατάστατος (*akatastatos*): restless; unstable; unsteady; up and down; anarchy

15. "ways" — ὁδός (*hodos*): road, path

16. [but] let — δέ (*de*): absolutely, categorically, emphatically

17. "rejoice" — καυχάομαι (*kauchaomai*): boast; boast confidently about something

18. "exalted" — ὕψος (*hupsos*): elevated position; high station

19. "rich" — πλούσιος (*plousios*): someone who possesses extreme wealth and enormous affluence

20. "flower" — ἄνθος (*anthos*): a bright flower; a blossoming flower

21. "pass away" — παρέρχομαι (*parerchomai*): pass by; come and go

22. "falleth" — ἐκπίπτω (*ekpipto*): to fall off; petals that loosen and fall off; to lose

23. "blessed" — μακάριος (*makarios*): supremely blessed; ridiculously blessed

24. "endureth" — ὑπομονή (*hupomone*): pictures defiantly sticking it out regardless of pressures mounted against it; staying power; "hang-in-there" power; the attitude that holds out, holds on, outlasts, perseveres, and hangs in there, never giving up, refusing to surrender to obstacles, and turning down every opportunity to quit; pictures one who is under a heavy load, but refuses to bend, break, or surrender

25. "temptation" — πειρασμός (*peirasmos*): to test, try, or tempt; to cause one to fail, to falter, to stumble, or to bring destruction; depicts a

calculated test to bring about failure; used to denote the actions of the devil, the tempter, or of the Pharisees and Sadducees

26. "crown of life" — στέφανον τῆς ζωῆς (*stephanon tes zoes*): a victor's crown; in ancient games, a laurel wreath was placed on the head of winning athletes; an athlete who obtained a victor's crown was esteemed and honored the rest of his life; the laurel wreath was a guarantee also of life-long provision

SYNOPSIS

Have you ever wondered what the Bible means when it says we are to "ask in faith"? Are there certain words we need to use and others we are to omit from our prayers? Is there a particular posture we are to take or a certain number of times we are required to pray in order to prove that we are really "asking in faith" and trusting God to provide for us? James addressed this issue in the opening chapter of his letter to the believers who had been driven out of Jerusalem and scattered throughout the Roman Empire as a result of great persecution.

The emphasis of this lesson:

If we need wisdom for anything, God will give it to us generously — without judging us or pointing out our faults. His one stipulation to receiving wisdom is that we come alongside Him in fellowship and ask for what we need in faith. If we continually waver in our faith, we are doubleminded and unstable and can't receive anything from God. But if we hold tightly to His promises and endure testing with the strength He gives, our lives will be truly blessed!

God Gives Us Wisdom
Liberally and Without Finding Fault

Have you ever felt like you were doing all that you knew to do, but you still weren't seeing the manifestation of God's promises in your life? That is how many believers in the Early Church felt when they were being persecuted and had been driven from their homes. They came to James, who was their pastor, and asked him why they were experiencing the hardships that were taking place. Of course, he didn't have all the answers, so he pointed them to the One who did and said:

If any of you lack wisdom, let him ask of God, that giveth to all men liberally, and upbraideth not; and it shall be given.
— James 1:5

We saw in our previous lesson that the word "of" is very important. When James says, "…Let him ask *of* God," the word "of" is the Greek word *para*, which means *alongside*. This word tells us God's one stipulation to receiving wisdom regarding our situation and that is we come alongside (*para*) Him. If we will draw close to God and come alongside Him, we will discover that He is the God of the open hand — not the God of a clenched fist.

Sadly, some Christians mistakenly believe that God is holding out on them. They think He is sitting up in Heaven taunting and teasing us, saying things like, "You're getting warmer… You're getting closer… You're red hot! You almost have it, and if you'll beg just a little bit more I'll tell you what you want to know." But God is *nothing* like that.

James said, "If you will come alongside (*para*) God and ask Him for the wisdom you need, you'll discover He is the God that giveth to all men liberally." In the Greek, this verse actually says, "Ask of the giving God," or, "Ask of the God that giveth." That is the God we serve — the open-handed God who gives "to all men liberally."

The phrase "to all" is the Greek word *pasin*, which means *to all* and is an all-inclusive term with *no exceptions*. This means if you come alongside (*para*) God, He will give you the wisdom you need "liberally." In Greek, this word "liberally" is *haplos*, and it describes *something given generously, abundantly, plentifully, profusely, bountifully*, and *open-handedly*. Moreover, it is *something provided copiously, amply, extravagantly, lavishly, liberally, plentifully*, or *richly*. This is the way you can expect God to answer you when you draw near to Him.

Equally important is the wonderful fact that He "upbraideth not." This word "upbraideth" in Greek is the word *oneididzo*, which means *to nitpick*. When you come alongside God for help, you don't have to worry or be afraid that He's going to judge you or condemn you and point out all your faults and weaknesses. *He is not a nitpicker.* He will give you the wisdom you need if you will humble yourself and draw near to Him.

We Need To 'Ask in Faith'

James goes on to say, "But let him ask in faith, nothing wavering. For he that wavereth is like a wave of the sea driven with the wind and tossed" (James 1:6). There is so much packed into this verse. Even the word "but" that opens the passage is significant. It is the little Greek word *de*, and here it serves as a marker to indicate something important. It is the equivalent of James saying, "*However, if you're going to ask God for wisdom, here's the way you need to ask.*" This word *de* is like an exclamation point to get our attention.

The word "ask" is also important. It is the Greek word *aiteo*, and it means *to request, to petition, or to demand*. This word was often used to describe the relationship between a parent and a child. Because of the child's status as a dependent, he has the right to ask his parent for what he needs, and the parent is obligated to answer. In fact, the word *aiteo*, (ask) is so strong it means *to ask with full expectation of receiving what was firmly requested*.

A great example of this word *aiteo* is found in Mark 15:43 where it says that Joseph of Arimathea "...went boldly unto Pilate, and *craved* the body of Jesus." The word "craved" here is the Greek word *aiteo*, which means Joseph *strongly requested* — even *demanded* — Jesus' body with the full expectation he would receive it so that he could give the Lord a proper burial, and he received what he asked for.

In the same way, James is telling his readers — including *us* — if we go to God and ask for something, we have to ask with a full expectation that we're going to receive what we're asking for. Specifically, he said we are to ask "in faith." The word "in" here is the Greek word *en*, which means *being rooted in* or *from a position of being in* faith.

Faith Does Not 'Waver'

The next thing James tells us in verse 6 is quite unique. Rather than explain how faith acts, he tells us how faith *doesn't* act. He says we are to ask in faith, "...nothing wavering. For he that wavereth is like a wave of the sea driven with the wind and tossed" (James 1:6). The word "wavering" here describes *habitual vacillation*. It is a picture of one going back and forth, changing his mind all the time.

With regards to prayer, it depicts a person who prays for something, and the next day he abandons that request altogether and prays for something else. Then a day or two later, he returns back to his original request and begins to ask God for it again. This on-again, off-again, flip-flop pattern of prayer is the type of wavering James said is not faith.

Faith stands solidly on the promises of God. It doesn't waver back and forth. Faith knows what it wants and will not stop asking for it until it is received. The one who wavers, James said, "...is like a wave of the sea driven with the wind and tossed" (James 1:6). The word "wave" here is the Greek word *kludoni*, and it describes *one wave after another wave* or *a succession of rising and falling waves*.

If you've ever been to the ocean, you've probably watched the waves. Looking out over the waters, you can see them as they build and grow bigger and bigger until finally, they peak and then fall, flattening out back into the sea from which they came. As you continue to watch, waves continue to form — gathering height, volume, and speed. Once more they rise and grow bigger and bigger until they finally peak and fall apart back into the sea from which they came.

Over and over, this never-ending process continues, giving us a vivid picture of a person who does not pray in faith. Oh, he *sounds* like he has impressive faith, but after a while he peaks and then changes his mind. When he changes his mind, he falls back into a maze of confusion where he rethinks what he's asking for. Then he rises up again and begins to ask for what he prayed before. It seems like he's really gaining strength and moving in faith, but then something happens and he changes his mind once more and returns to the maze of confusion and doubt.

James said this type of person is "driven with the wind." This phrase is a translation of the Greek word *anemidzo*, and it means *driven along by the push of the wind* or *agitated and stirred up by the movement of wind*. James said this person who is wavering in faith is also "tossed," which in Greek is the word *rhipidzo*, meaning *constantly or habitually rising and falling*. Thus, a person who is wavering in their faith is just like the ever-changing positions of waves in the sea.

One Who Wavers in Faith Is 'Doubleminded'

God has a name for the person who habitually vacillates back and forth in their faith. He says that person is "doubleminded." The Bible tells us,

"For let not that man think that he shall receive any thing of the Lord. A double minded man is unstable in all his ways" (James 1:7,8).

In Greek, the term "doubleminded" is *dipsuchos*, which literally means *two-souled*. The implication here is that a person who is doubleminded is *one with two heads*; one head says to do one thing, and the other head says just the opposite. It is a picture of one who vacillates back and forth constantly.

James uses the word *dipsuchos* ("doubleminded") to paint a picture of what some people look like when they pray — like a man with two heads, speaking two different things. God wants to bless us, but trying to bless someone who is doubleminded is like trying to hit a moving target. It is only when you ask in faith without wavering that your faith becomes a stationary target God can easily hit.

Furthermore, the Bible says a doubleminded man is "unstable in all his ways." The word "unstable" is a translation of the Greek word *akatastatos*, which means *restless; unstable; unsteady;* or *up and down*. It is actually the term from where we get the word *anarchy*. When a person is unstable in his or her faith, it means that person is not consistently focused on what he or she is praying for, which will eventually produce *anarchy* throughout that person's life.

James 1:8 declares, "A double minded man is unstable in all his ways." The word "ways" is a translation of the Greek word *hodos*, which is the word for *a road* or *path*. Eventually, the instability in a person will begin to seep into and affect *every road of life* on which he walks. If he remains unstable, anarchy and destruction will begin to surface in his life. Hopefully you are beginning to see how important it is to stick with what you believe.

When You Hit Rock-Bottom, Rejoice for the Promotion Ahead

James goes on to say, "Let the brother of low degree rejoice in that he is exalted" (James 1:9). It's interesting to note that in the original Greek text, the word "but" appears as the first word of this verse. It says, "*But* let the brother...." This word "but" is the Greek word *de*, which means *absolutely, categorically,* or *emphatically*. It indicates that James is exclaiming *emphatically* and *categorically*, "[But] let the brother of low degree rejoice in that he is exalted" (James 1:9).

The word "brother" is again the Greek word *adelphos*, which James used at the opening of his letter. It was a term used to describe *two or more who were born from the same womb*. This word was made popular by Alexander the Great and later used in a military sense to depict *brothers in battle* or a *comrade*. Thus, a brother of low degree is one who has been greatly humbled and his self-importance reduced. James said this humble comrade should "rejoice."

In Greek, the word "rejoice" is *kauchaomai*, and it means *to boast confidently about something*. What is he to boast about? James said, "...That he is exalted" (James 1:9). The word "exalted" is the Greek word *hupsos*, and it describes *an elevated position* or *high station in life*. Remember, James is writing to believers who are suffering great persecution. Essentially, he is telling them, "If you've hit rock bottom, *rejoice* because you're on your way up to an elevated, higher position!"

A Man's Life and His Wealth
Rapidly Fade Like Short-Lived Flowers

When we come to James 1:10, he adds, "But the rich, in that he is made low: because as the flower of the grass he shall pass away." The word "rich" here is the Greek word *plousios*, and it describes *wealth so great it cannot be tabulated*. It is a picture of *abundant or vast wealth*; *extreme riches*; *unlimited wealth*; or *abundance*. It depicts *someone who possesses extreme wealth and enormous affluence*.

Here James is basically saying, "If you've attained everything and feel you can't go any higher; then you've come to the reality that life is short, and eventually everything passes away." That's why he compares a person's life to a "flower" — the Greek word *anthos*, which describes *a blossoming flower*. As bright and as beautiful a flower is, it is fleeting and will soon "pass away." The phrase "pass away" is from the Greek word *parerchomai*, meaning *to pass by, to come and go,* or *to perish*. No matter how much wealth and prestige a person acquires, it will quickly come and go in the light of eternity.

James continues his discussion on the brevity of life in verse 11, saying, "For the sun is no sooner risen with a burning heat, but it withereth the grass, and the flower thereof falleth, and the grace of the fashion of it perisheth: so also shall the rich man fade away in his ways" (James 1:11).

Again, we see the comparison of a person's life and his wealth with a blossoming "flower" (*anthos*), which is here today and gone tomorrow.

The words "burning heat" are a translation of the Greek word *kauson*, which describes *a hot wind that passes over and dries up everything*. This "burning heat" causes the flower to "falleth," which in Greek means *to fall off* and describes *the petals that loosen and fall off one by one*. James is basically telling us that what we see and observe with our eyes — which is what the word "fashion" refers to — is quickly fading away. No matter how wealthy a person is, at the end of his life, it matters not because everything will "fade away." This is a translation of the Greek word *maraino* and means *his life will become depleted little by little* — even in the middle of his pursuits.

The One Who Endures Temptation Is Truly 'Blessed'

James circles back to refocus our attention on what matters most by saying, "Blessed is the man that endureth temptation: for when he is tried, he shall receive the crown of life, which the Lord hath promised to them that love him" (James 1:12). The word "blessed" here is the Greek word *makarios*, and it means *supremely blessed* or *ridiculously blessed*. It specifically refers to being blessed as a result of receiving God's provisions.

Who does James say is blessed by God so lavishly? It's the person that "endureth temptation." The word "endureth" is the Greek word *hupomone* — the same word translated as "patience" in verses 3 and 4. Again, the word *hupomone* pictures *one who defiantly sticks it out regardless of pressures mounted against him*. It depicts *staying power* or *"hang-in- there" power*. It is *the attitude that holds out, holds on, outlasts, perseveres, and hangs in there, never giving up, refusing to surrender to obstacles, and turning down every opportunity to quit*. It is the picture of one who is under a heavy load, but refuses to bend, break, or surrender.

James describes the heavy load being endured as "temptation" — the Greek word *peirasmos*. This word depicts *a calculated test to bring about failure*, and it is used in Scripture particularly to denote the actions of the devil, the tempter, or of the Pharisees and Sadducees. It means *to test, try, or tempt in order to cause one to fail, to falter, to stumble, or to bring destruction*.

To be clear, it is the enemy — not God — that brings "temptation." It is Satan that wants your soul to be "tried." In Greek, the word "tried" is *dokimos*, which means *to pass a scrutinizing test*. It is the picture of *one who is tested, approved, and received as genuine.* After a scrutinizing examination, this person's character has been validated and verified, and they have been deemed "fit" for advancement.

James tells us that the one who endures temptation and passes the test, "…He shall receive the crown of life, which the Lord hath promised to them that love him" (James 1:12). The phrase "crown of life" in Greek is *stephanon tes zoes*, and it describes *a victor's crown*. In ancient games, a laurel wreath was placed on the head of winning athletes, and an athlete who obtained a victor's crown was esteemed and honored for the rest of his life. Furthermore, the laurel wreath was also a guarantee of life-long provision for its recipient.

That's why this person is *supremely and ridiculously blessed!* One who successfully overcomes the trials and tests of life secures the key to receiving whatever he needs for the rest of his life. Are you beginning to see why it is crucial that you learn how to stay in a place of faith and not habitually vacillate like the waves of the sea? Why not make the decision today that you're going to hold tightly to the promises of God and not budge? Surrender your life afresh to Him right now and receive His supernatural, "hang-in-there" (*hupomene*) empowerment!

STUDY QUESTIONS

Study to shew thyself approved unto God, a workman that needeth not to be ashamed, rightly dividing the word of truth.
— 2 Timothy 2:15

1. According to James 4:2 and 3, why do we sometimes not have what we need and why do our prayers sometimes go unanswered? What does Psalm 145:17-20 say is required for God to hear and answer our prayers?

2. James 1:6 says if we need something from God, we are to "ask in faith." The word "ask" is the strong Greek word *aiteo*, which means *to ask with full expectation of receiving what was firmly requested.* Did you ever stop and think about how important your expectations are — and that God has expectations too? Carefully consider these words from the prophet Isaiah:

    "And therefore the Lord [earnestly] waits [expecting, looking, and longing] to be gracious to you; and therefore He lifts Himself up, that He may have mercy on you and show loving-kindness to you. For the Lord is a God of justice. Blessed (happy, fortunate, to be envied) are all those who [earnestly] wait for Him, who expect and look and long for Him [for His victory, His favor, His love, His peace, His joy, and His matchless unbroken companionship]!"

— Isaiah 30:18 (*AMPC*)

What is God speaking to you about expectations in this rich passage?

1. In and of itself, money and material possessions are not sinful. It is *the love of* money that is the root of all evil. Take time to look up the following passages. What should you keep in mind regarding…

   • **Wealth and material possessions?** Proverbs 23:4,5; 1 Timothy 6:6-12; Hebrews 13:5

   • **The time you've been given?** Psalm 90:5,6,12; James 4:13-15; Ephesians 5:15-17; 1 Corinthians 7:29-31

PRACTICAL APPLICATION

But be ye doers of the word, and not hearers only,
deceiving your own selves.
— James 1:22

1. In your own words, briefly describe what it means to "ask in faith" and not *waver in faith* like a wave of the sea that is driven and tossed by the wind. Be honest with yourself. Would you say that your behavior confirms that you're in faith or that you're doubleminded like a man with two heads?

2. What do you know you need to do differently to strengthen your faith and stop vacillating in what you are believing God for?

3. Take a few minutes to reflect on James 1:9-11. Why do you think God prompted James to write about the brevity of life and the fleetingness of riches to people who were experiencing persecution? What do these verses speak to you personally about your own life in the light of eternity? Is there anything you need to reprioritize? If so, what is it?

TOPIC

What God Gives and Never Gives

SCRIPTURES

1. **James 1:1** — James, a servant of God and of the Lord Jesus Christ, to the twelve tribes which are scattered abroad, greeting.

2. **James 1:13-17** — Let no man say when he is tempted, I am tempted of God: for God cannot be tempted with evil, neither tempteth he any man: But every man is tempted, when he is drawn away of his own lust, and enticed. Then when lust hath conceived, it bringeth forth sin: and sin, when it is finished, bringeth forth death. Do not err, my beloved brethren. Every good gift and every perfect gift is from above, and cometh down from the Father of lights, with whom is no variableness, neither shadow of turning.

GREEK WORDS

1. "scattered abroad" — **διασπορά** (*diaspora*): the random scattering of seed; used to depict the scattering of Jewish believers

2. "tempted" — **πειράζω** (*peiradzo*): to test, try, or tempt; to cause one to fail, to falter, to stumble, or to bring destruction; depicts a calculated test to bring about failure; used to denote the actions of the devil, the tempter, or of the Pharisees and Sadducees

3. "of" — **ἀπὸ** (*apo*): away from; denotes something done from a distance or something done remotely

4. "evil" — **κακός** (*kakos*): evil, vile, foul, or destructive

5. "drawn away" — **ἐξέλκω** (*exelko*): to lure; to induce

6. "enticed" — **δελεάζω** (*deleadzo*): to bait a hook; to set a trap with bait; to entice a victim into a trap

7. "conceived" — **συλλαμβάνω** (*sullambano*): to conceive; to become pregnant

8. "brings forth" — **ἀποκυέω** (*apokueo*): a medical term indicating the close of pregnancy; full process of pregnancy from conception, to delivery, to maturity

9. "death" — θάνατος (*thanatos*): spiritual death; a execution verdict
10. "err" — πλανάω (*planao*): to wander off-track; to veer from the right path; to lose one's way
11. "good" — ἀγαθός (*agathos*): anything good, beneficial, or profitable
12. "gift" — δόσις (*dosis*): perpetual giving from God; the habitual giving of God
13. "perfect" — τέλειον (*teleion*): mature, complete, perfect, perfecting
14. "from above" — ἄνωθεν (*anothen*): from a higher realm; from above; from heaven
15. "cometh down" — καταβαίνω (*katabaino*): to be dominated by something coming down very hard, like a downpour of rain
16. "with whom" — παρ' ᾧ (*par oo*): alongside of him

SYNOPSIS

James opens his letter, identifying who he is and who he is writing to. He says, "James, a servant of God and of the Lord Jesus Christ, to the twelve tribes which are scattered abroad, greeting" (James 1:1). We noted in Lesson 2 that the phrase "scattered abroad" is the Greek word *diaspora*, and it describes *the random scattering of seed*. This word was used here to depict *the scattering of Jewish believers*.

Like seed seized by the hand of the sower, they were ripped out of their homes and jobs and taken away from family and friends, and then randomly scattered all over the eastern lands of the Roman Empire without rhyme or reason. This tells us the dislocation of these believers was not nice, neat, or orderly; it was very disruptive and chaotic.

As a result of great persecution, they were experiencing devastation and pain in their lives. Confused and overwhelmed by the turn of events, believers from all across the Roman Empire wrote letters to James, asking him to explain why they were going through such crushing difficulties. If anyone could answer their questions it was James, the half-brother of Jesus and the most visible Jewish believer in the city of Jerusalem.

The emphasis of this lesson:

God cannot be tempted, neither does He tempt anyone. There is no evil in Him. If you think correctly and understand that the difficult situations you're facing are not from God, you'll fight against them. Right

thinking about trouble and trials is the first step to breaking free from the enemy's trap. Only good, beneficial, and maturing things come from God. This is a forever fact that never changes.

God Cannot Be Tempted
Neither Does He Tempt Anyone

We can determine from James' words what the dispersed believers were asking him. For instance, in James 1:13, he said, "Let no man say when he is tempted, I am tempted of God: for God cannot be tempted with evil, neither tempteth he any man." This response from James lets us know these distraught Christians were asking him, "Has God somehow or in some way mysteriously allowed all this tragedy to come into our lives? Is He tempting us?"

Notice the first four words out of James' mouth: "Let no man say...." In Greek, this is a very strong rebuke or prohibition that literally means, "I hear what you're saying, and I don't like it. Stop it and stop it now!" What were these believers saying? They were saying when they were tempted that they were being "tempted of God."

To this James said, "Let no man say when he is tempted, I am tempted of God..." (James 1:13). The word "tempted," which appears twice, is the Greek word *peiradzo*, and it means *to test, try, or tempt*. It describes Satan's consistent attempts to bring people down and destroy them. It also means *to cause one to fail, to falter, to stumble*, or *to bring destruction*. It is the very word used to describe the temptation Jesus experienced when He went without food for 40 days in the wilderness — when the devil did everything he could to derail Jesus from His place of faith and His purpose. It's also the word used in the gospels to describe the attacks brought against Jesus by the Pharisees and Sadducees. This word *peiradzo* depicts *a calculated test to bring about failure.*

Also notice the word "of." When James was writing this, he had two options he could have used for the word "of": he could have used the word *hupo* or the word *apo* because both would be translated as "of." But the word *hupo* would imply *direct agency*, which would have meant they were saying, "We know that God has *personally* sent all these tragic events into our lives." However, he didn't use the word *hupo*; he used the word *apo*.

In Greek, the word *apo* means *away from* and denotes *something done from a distance* or *something done remotely*. The use of *apo* here implies these Christians believed God was doing something remotely. They were beginning to believe that although He didn't personally, directly bring destruction into their lives, He did it from a distance.

"God is God," they were saying. "And if He had wanted to stop these hardships, He could have stopped them. So since He didn't stop them, it must be His permissive will for us to go through them." This type of thinking is wrong, and that is why James essentially told them, "Let no man say when he is tempted that God is causing it. How dare you say that! How can you even think that God would do such things to you? That is just not the nature of God!"

God Is Totally Void of Evil

James goes on to say, "...For God cannot be tempted with evil, neither tempteth he any man" (James 1:13). The word "evil" is the Greek word *kakos*, and it describes *something evil, vile, foul, or destructive*. God has no personal experience with "evil." He can't be tempted by it nor does He tempt people with it. When "evil" tried to come into Heaven in the person of Lucifer, God put a stop to it by casting Satan and those who rebelled with him out of His presence.

There is no evil in Heaven, and God doesn't bring evil into your life to test you. It is something He simply cannot do. If you think God permits evil to come into your life, you will remain in the evil trap of the enemy. However, if you think correctly and understand that the difficult situations you're facing are not sent from God, you will fight against them. Right thinking about trouble and trials is the first step to getting out of your trap.

Why Is Temptation So Powerful and Alluring?

Have you ever wondered why the temptations you face are so enticing? James shines a spotlight on the reason, saying, "But every man is tempted, when he is drawn away of his own lust, and enticed" (James 1:14). Again, the word "tempted" here is the Greek word *peiradzo*, which describes *a calculated test to bring about failure and release destruction in your life*. James says that every man enters a calculated test that is designed to make him stumble and fall "when he is drawn away of his own lust."

The words "drawn away" are a translation of the Greek word *exelko*, which means *to coax*, *to lure*, or *to induce*. Equally important is the word "enticed" — the Greek word *deleadzo* — which means *to bait a hook* or *to set a trap with bait*. It is the picture of enticing a victim into a trap. Satan — and his evil cohorts — are like a master fisherman who knows exactly what *lure* to throw out in front of you and how to make that lure come alive before your eyes. His goal is to lure you out of your safe place in Christ and get you to bite his bait so he can set his hooks into you and jerk you anywhere he wants you to go.

In this verse, James is speaking to believers who are being lured away into wrong thinking about God. The idea that God is tempting them — or allowing these devastating tests to come into their lives — is the lure Satan was dangling in front of them. They were entertaining and playing with wrong thoughts, and those thoughts were luring them away from God.

Friend, you need to be careful what you think about and focus on. You need to be mindful of what you're watching and listening to and who you're spending a lot of time with. As a believer, you are in Jesus Christ — He is your *safe place*. In Him, healing and deliverance and everything you need to live a life of victory belongs to you. But the devil will try to draw you out of that safe place by using just the right bait to lure you away. Don't believe and bite into his lies!

Believing Satan's Lies Will Give Birth to Sin and Death

James goes on to say, "Then when lust hath conceived, it bringeth forth sin: and sin, when it is finished, bringeth forth death" (James 1:15). The word "conceived" here is the Greek word *sullambano*, which literally means *to conceive* or *to become pregnant*. Here we learn that when we bite the enemy's bait, we conceive — or become pregnant — with sin.

Think about what needs to happen for a woman to get pregnant. In order for her to conceive a baby, she and her husband have to get *really close*. She can't become pregnant if she's in one room of the house and her husband is in another room. On the contrary, to conceive, they must be intimately connected.

Using this imagery, James is telling us that if we entertain wrong thoughts in our mind — focusing and fixating on them — eventually we're going to be impregnated with the enemy's lies. The next thing he tells us will happen is, "…It bringeth forth sin…" (James 1:15). The words "bringeth forth" is the Greek word *apokueo*, which is *a medical term indicating the close of pregnancy*. It depicts *the full process of pregnancy from conception, to delivery, to maturity*.

If you conceive a wrong thought in your head and you don't do something to stop it, it will produce something disastrous in your life. The Bible calls it *death* — the Greek word *thanatos*, which indicates *all kinds of bad things*. This word *thanatos* was used to describe *spiritual death* and is also the very same word used by the Greeks to describe *an execution verdict*. In other words, wrong thinking will kill you. This warning is echoed by the apostle Paul in Romans 8:6.

It's no wonder James issues the warning, "Do not err, my beloved brethren" (James 1:16). The word "err" here is the Greek work *planao*, which means *to wander off-track*; *to veer from the right path*; or *to lose one's way*. It is the same Greek word used to describe the great deception of the last days and the strong delusion that will come upon all those who reject God during the Tribulation. James is urging his readers — including *us* — not to bite the bait of thinking that God is the source of our troubles.

Only One Thing
Comes From God

Under the inspiration of the Holy Spirit, James makes this powerful declaration concerning the one thing — and *the only thing* — that comes from God: "Every good gift and every perfect gift is from above, and cometh down from the Father of lights, with whom is no variableness, neither shadow of turning" (James 1:17).

First he says every "good gift" comes from God. The word "good" is the Greek word *agathos*, which describes *anything good, beneficial, or profitable*. Basically, if something is good, it's from God. And the word "gift" in Greek is *dosis*, which describes how God gives — *perpetually* and *habitually*. The word *dosis*, translated "gift," informs us that God doesn't just give a single gift; He keeps on giving and giving and giving. And everything He gives is *good, beneficial*, and *profitable*.

In addition to God's gifts being good, the Bible says they are also "perfect." This is a translation of the Greek word *teleion*, which describes *something mature, complete, perfect*, or *perfecting*. This means we could translate this verse, *"Every good habitual giving of God is completing, maturing, and perfecting."* If we receive something from God, it *never takes away* — it *always adds to us*. What God gives perfects and completes us.

Does cancer add to your life or take away? What about other forms of sickness or disease, such as arthritis, Parkinson's disease, leukemia, migraines, and infertility? Do they add to your life or take away? Therefore, none of these is from God. Only "good and perfect gifts" come from above. Every deadly, damaging, and destructive thing is from below.

God Desires To Disperse A Downpour of His Blessings

The phrase "from above" is the Greek word *anothen*, and it means *from a higher realm, from above*, or *from heaven*. When the Bible says these gifts "cometh down," it uses the Greek word *katabaino*, which is a compound of the words *kata* and *baino*. The word *kata* describes *something that comes down so hard it is dominating or subjugating*; and the word *baino* means *to step down*. It is the same word one would use to describe walking down a flight of stairs. When the words *kata* and *baino* are compounded to form *katabaino*, it means *to be dominated or subjugated by something coming down very hard, like a downpour of rain*.

Have you ever been driving in a downpour, and the rain was coming down so hard and heavy that you couldn't see anything in front of you? Sometimes the downpour is so dominating that you have to pull over to the side of the road and wait for the rain to stop. That is a picture of what the phrase "cometh down" means, and it indicates how God is sending His good and perfect gifts to you.

Someone may say, "If God is pouring good and perfect gifts on me, why am I not hit by one of those downpours at least occasionally?" The answer is simple — you must receive His gifts by faith. If your mind thinks and believes that God is causing or allowing your problems, you're not looking for or anticipating His goodness to pour into your life. If this is the way you've been seeing God, you have work to renew your mind and conform your thoughts with the truth.

As you begin believing for and expecting "good and perfect gifts" to come into your life, you put yourself in position to receive from the "Father of lights" instead of receiving from the father of darkness — the devil.

When It Comes To Giving, There's No Changing in What He Provides

Take note of how James describes God. Instead of just saying, "Every good and every perfect gift is from God," he uses comparative language and says, "Every good gift and every perfect gift is from above, and cometh down from the Father of lights, with whom is no variableness, neither shadow of turning" (James 1:17).

The words "with whom" are very important. In Greek, it is *par oo*, and it means *alongside of him*. This means if you could get right up next to God and look into His very being, you would clearly see that when it comes to the issue of what He gives and what He never gives, nothing ever changes. That is why James said there is "no variableness, neither shadow of turning" with God.

These words describe the shifting shadows of a Roman sundial. As time passes and the sun moves across the sky, the sundial casts a shadow that tells the time of day. As the sun moves, the shadow on the sundial shifts to reflect the accurate time. This means every time you look at a sundial, the shadow has changed and is still changing. It is technically never the same.

By describing God as "the Father of lights, with whom is no variableness, neither shadow of turning," James is saying, "God is *not* like a Roman sundial with regards to what He gives you. There is no variableness or changing in what He provides. What comes from Him is always a steady flow of good and perfect gifts."

That means when tragedy comes, you don't need to stop and wonder if it is from God or the enemy. You don't even need to stop and pray about it. Anything that enters your life to bring damage, destruction, or ruin is from the devil — *not* God. But if what comes to you is good, beneficial, completing, and perfecting, it is from God. If what you're experiencing takes away from your life, it is from the devil. If it adds to your life, it's from God. On this issue of what God gives and what He never gives, there is no variableness or shadow of turning. He never changes! If you know this and believe this, you will know what things to receive and what things to resist.

STUDY QUESTIONS

Study to shew thyself approved unto God, a workman that needeth not to be ashamed, rightly dividing the word of truth.
— 2 Timothy 2:15

1. Are there temptations you're facing on a regular basis that seem to be extremely difficult to resist? What does the devil keep dangling in front of your eyes that seems so alluring and desirable? Reread James 1:14,15. What new insights regarding temptation is the Holy Spirit showing you? (Also consider James 4:1-10.)

2. It is vital to guard your heart and mind and not give the enemy any ammunition to use against you. Take time to meditate on these powerful truths and write down any action steps God brings to mind that you can take to safeguard yourself from becoming a victim of temptation.

   Let your way in life be far from her {sexual temptation}, and come not near the door of her house [avoid the very scenes of temptation] (Proverbs 5:8 *AMPC*).

   Jesus said, "I will not talk with you much more, for the prince (evil genius, ruler) of the world is coming. And he has no claim on Me. [He has nothing in common with Me; there is nothing in Me that belongs to him, and he has no power over Me]" (John 14:30 *AMPC*.)

   No temptation has come your way that is too hard for flesh and blood to bear. But God can be trusted not to allow you to suffer any temptation beyond your powers of endurance. He will see to it that every temptation has its way out, so that it will be possible for you to bear it. (1 Corinthians 10:13 *J.B. Phillips*).

   For because He Himself {Jesus} [in His humanity] has suffered in being tempted (tested and tried), He is able [immediately] to run to the cry of (assist, relieve) those who are being tempted and tested and tried [and who therefore are being exposed to suffering] (Hebrews 2:18 *AMPC*).

PRACTICAL APPLICATION

But be ye doers of the word, and not hearers only,
deceiving your own selves.
— James 1:22

1. As you come to the conclusion of this eye-opening series, what is your greatest takeaway — what truth do you want the Holy Spirit to forever seal in your heart and mind?

2. Like the distraught believers in the Early Church, have you thought or said, "Is God somehow or in some way allowing this tragedy to come into my life? Is it His permissive will that I experience the hardship and heartache I'm facing?" How is this lesson helping you see that this way of thinking is a deadly trap of the enemy?

3. The Bible declares, "Every good gift and every perfect gift is from above..." (James 1:17). What comes from God *never takes away* — it *always adds to us*. In light of this truth, what things are you dealing with that you thought were from God, but now know they are not?

4. Take a moment and pray: *Lord, is there anything I'm watching and/or listening to that is filling my mind and heart with wrong thoughts about You and Your Word? Is there anyone I'm hanging out with that is polluting and poisoning my perspective? Please show me and give me the desire and power to remove anything that is luring me away from You. In Jesus' name. Amen.*"

Notes